Published By: North Parade Publishing Ltd.
4 North Parade, Bath, BA1 1LF, UK

CONTENTS

THE EARTH

The **Earth** is the only planet in the solar system known to support life. Land covers only a third of the Earth's surface with water and ice covering the rest.

Different continents and oceans

Land is divided into seven main parts called continents. They are Asia, Africa, North America, South America, Antarctica, Europe and Australia. Similarly, there are five major water bodies called Oceans. They are the Pacific Ocean, Atlantic Ocean, Indian Ocean, Southern Ocean and Arctic Ocean.

Mt. Everest — the highest place on Earth.

It's hot in there

The continents and the oceans make up the outside or the crust of the Earth. The inside of the Earth's surface however, is made up of a huge ball of hot but solid rock. It is because of this that the temperature at the Earth's center is believed to be about 8,100° Fahrenheit or 4,500° Celsius!

The Mid-Ocean Ridge

The Earth's longest mountain range is the underwater Mid-Ocean Ridge. It's more than 31,069 miles (50,000 km) long and winds around the globe from the Arctic Ocean to the Atlantic, skirting Africa, Asia and Australia, and crossing the Pacific to the west coast of North America. It is four times longer than the **Andes**, **Rockies**, and **Himalayas** combined.

The Sahara — the world's biggest sand desert.

DID YOU KNOW ?

The Earth is over 4.5 billion years old!

The Dead Sea — the lowest point on Earth.

CANADA AND THE USA

Canada is geographically bigger than the United States, but the latter is nine times more populated.

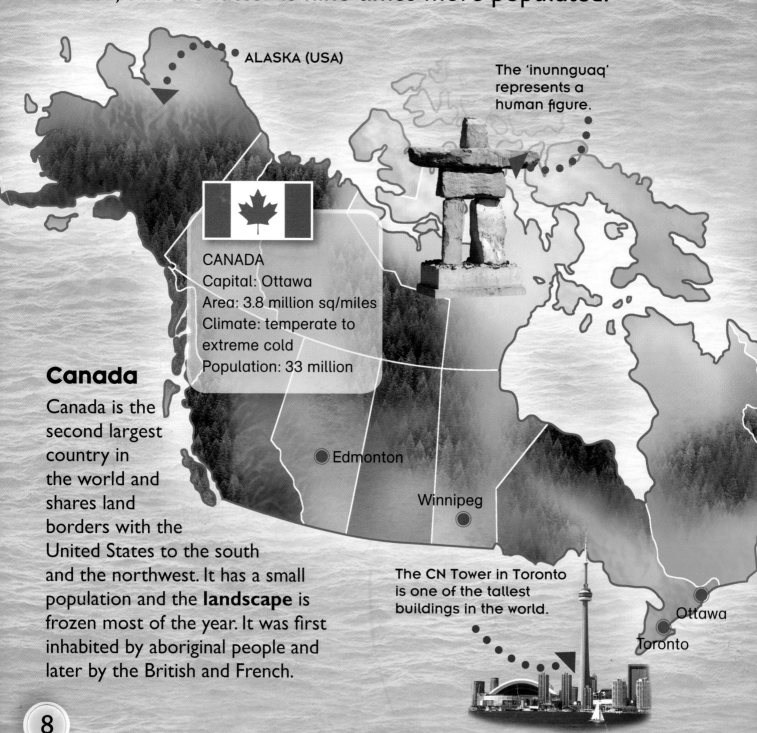

ALASKA (USA)

The 'inunnguaq' represents a human figure.

CANADA
Capital: Ottawa
Area: 3.8 million sq/miles
Climate: temperate to extreme cold
Population: 33 million

Canada

Canada is the second largest country in the world and shares land borders with the United States to the south and the northwest. It has a small population and the **landscape** is frozen most of the year. It was first inhabited by aboriginal people and later by the British and French.

Edmonton

Winnipeg

The CN Tower in Toronto is one of the tallest buildings in the world.

Ottawa

Toronto

United States of America

The United States of America is a huge country with 50 states. The country is situated mostly in central North America, with Washington, D.C. as its capital. The United States lies between the Pacific and Atlantic Oceans, bordered by Canada to the north and Mexico to the south. The country is regarded as the most powerful nation in the world with lots of **natural resources.**

The Statue of Liberty in New York was gifted to the US by France.

United States of America
Capital: Washington, D.C.
Area: 3.5 million sq/miles
Climate: mostly temperate
Population: 307 million

Seattle

Denver

Los Angeles

Chicago

Washington, D.C.

Dallas

Alaska

Alaska is the country's biggest state, but also the least dense in terms of population. It once belonged to Russia, before the US purchased it in 1867 for $7.2 million!

Fun Facts

The venus fly trap only lives in the wild in the Carolinas and nowhere else in the world.

DID YOU KNOW?

Basketball was invented by a Canadian named Dr. James Naismith. He invented the game while working in Boston with college students.

MEXICO AND CENTRAL AMERICA

Mexico and Central America form a natural bridge linking the United States with South America. The culturally rich region is full of ancient, historical ruins.

Mexico

Mexico is famous for its culture, especially the largely untouched ruins of the Mayan civilization. This country of over 100 million is full of natural splendor – from the lovely plains and mountains to its beautiful coastline.

Nicaragua

Nicaragua is the largest Central American country. Its history is tainted by civil wars, and volcanoes and earthquakes are always a threat to this country. However, it has its share of natural attractions. The coral reefs and the mangrove forests are rich with flora and fauna, and are a big hit with tourists.

MEXICO
Capital: Mexico City
Area: 741 million sq/miles
Climate: tropical to desert
Population: 111 million

Fun Facts

Mexico City hosted the nineteenth Olympic Games in 1968. It is the only Latin America country to do so. It has also hosted the FIFA World Cup twice, in 1970 and 1986.

Costa Rica

Costa Rica is located between the Pacific Ocean and the Caribbean Sea. Its picturesque landscape makes this small country an ideal tourist destination. Costa Rica literally translates as 'rich coast' and the country is known for its coffee production.

Chichen Itza in Mexico — remains of the mighty Maya civilization.

Mexico City

Belmopan

BELIZE
Capital: Belmopan
Area: 8,805 sq/miles
Climate: tropical
Population: 307,000

Guatemala City

Belize

Belize is located on the Caribbean coast of Central America. The landscape is sprinkled with Maya ruins and **diverse** animal life, ranging from the jaguar to the toucan monkey. Belize also has the Western Hemisphere's longest coral reef.

Since 1828, the Poas volcano in Costa Rica has erupted 39 times.

COSTA RICA
Capital: San Jose
Area: 19,559 sq/miles
Climate: tropical and subtropical
Population: 4.2 million

Managua

San Jose

DID YOU KNOW?

Guatemala is the original homeland of the Maya civilization, which flourished from circa 2,000 BC to 250 AD.

NORTH ANDEAN COUNTRIES

North Andean countries include Ecuador, Bolivia, Peru and Colombia.

A colorful market in Otavolo, Ecuador.

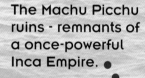

COLOMBIA
Capital: Bogota
Area: 398,000 sq/miles
Climate: tropical to cool
Population: 45 million

Bogota

Quito

The Machu Picchu ruins - remnants of a once-powerful Inca Empire.

Peru

Peru is the largest country in South America after Brazil and Argentina. It is unique for having three different landscapes – the rocky Andes, the Atacama Desert, and the Amazonian forest.

Lima

PERU
Capital: Lima
Area: 494,000 sq/miles
Climate: diverse (tropical to cool)
Population: 29 million

Colombia

Colombia is the only country to touch both the Atlantic and the Pacific oceans. Colombia is famous for its jewelry, especially its emeralds. It is also known for having the continent's highest coal production. The climate is tropical because of its proximity to the equator, but there are peaks that are covered in snow owing to the altitude.

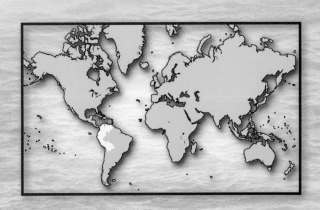

Ecuador

Ecuador is located on the northwestern corner of the South American continent. It has Colombia to its north, and Peru to the southeast. The Galapagos Islands are a part of Ecuador, and the country has some of the greatest **biodiversity** of any country in the world. The climate is mostly tropical, with an extreme rainy season.

ECUADOR
Capital: Quito
Area: 106,888 sq/miles
Climate: mostly tropical
Population: 14.5 million

Fun Facts

The Galapagos volcanoes, 597 miles (960 km) west of Ecuador, bring a lot of tourists to the country because of their unique and diverse flora and fauna.

The Andes

The Andes mountain range dominates the west of the South American continent and is one of the longest mountain ranges in the world. It is over 4,400 miles (7,000 km) long, and 300 miles (700 km) at its widest. The average height of its mountains is about 13,000 ft (4000 m).

DID YOU KNOW?

The word Peru in the Quechua language means 'land of abundance'.

BRAZIL AND NEIGHBORING COUNTRIES

Brazil is South America's biggest country. Its neighbors include Argentina, Peru, Paraguay, Colombia, Venezuela, Suriname, Guyana, and Bolivia.

Guyana

Originally a Dutch colony in the 17th century, by 1815 Guyana had come under British rule. It is also one of the four non-Spanish-speaking territories on the continent, along with the states of Brazil (Portuguese) and Suriname (Dutch), and the French overseas region of French Guiana (French).

VENEZUELA
Capital: Caracas
Area: 340,561 sq/miles
Climate: tropical and moderate
Population: 27 million

TRINIDAD AND TOBAGO
Capital: Port of Spain
Area: 1,981 sq/miles
Climate: tropical
Population: 1.2 million

The Itaipu dam is the world's most powerful electricity generating station.

Trinidad and Tobago

The islands of Trinidad and Tobago may be close to each other, but have their own distinctive cultural flavors. Trinidad, mainly inhabited by people of African and Indian descent, is known for its steel music. Tobago, the smaller of the two islands, is slower paced and more scenic.

Suriname

Suriname is home to the Maroons – descendants of African slaves who arrived about 300 years back. Its capital is Paramaribo.

Port of Spain

Caracas

Georgetown

Paramaribo

Cayenne

GUYANA
Capital: Georgetown
Area: 76,004 sq/miles
Climate: tropical
Population: 772,000

BRAZIL
Capital: Brasilia
Area: 3.26 million sq/miles
Climate: mostly tropical
Population: 199 million

Brazil

Brazil is the largest country in the continent occupying nearly half of South America. Brazil is also the fifth most populated country and the fourth most populated democracy in the world. Football is the national sport and is followed religiously.

Brasilia

Fun Facts

The Statue of Christ, the 130 ft tall statue that overlooks Rio de Janeiro, is one of the seven wonders of modern times. This sculpture is the symbol and icon of Brazil.

The Statue of Christ, Rio de Janeiro, Brazil.

DID YOU KNOW?

Venezuela has the largest proven oil reserves outside the Middle East. Also, besides the US, it has the largest natural gas reserves.

ARGENTINA AND NEIGHBORING COUNTRIES

Argentina borders Paraguay and Bolivia to the north, Brazil and Uruguay to the northeast, and Chile to the west and south.

La Paz

La Paz, Bolivia, is the highest capital city in the world.

Argentina

Argentina is the second largest country in South America and eighth in the world. The country's culture is heavily shaped by the Europeans, most particularly the Italians and Spanish people, who formed the largest percentage of newcomers from 1860 to 1930.

ARGENTINA
Capital: Buenos Aires
Area: 1.05 million sq/miles
Climate: mostly temperate
Population: 41 million

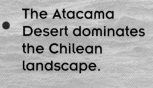

The Atacama Desert dominates the Chilean landscape.

Uruguay

Uruguay is located in the southeastern part of the continent and is typified by low grasslands. It has the highest literacy rate and the lowest poverty rate in the continent and education is compulsory and free. The economy of the country is dominated by agriculture.

Chile

Chile is 2,485 miles (4,000 km) long and only 93 miles (150 km) wide on average. Eighty percent of the country is covered by mountains. People are mostly of European descent or a mixture of European and **indigenous** ancestry. In the Atacama desert lie the Chuquicamata and Escondida copper mines.

Asuncion

PARAGUAY
Capital: Asuncion
Area: 153,398 sq/miles
Climate: subtropical to temperate
Population: 7 million

CHILE
Capital: Santiago
Area: 289,113 sq/miles
Climate: Diverse (temperate to cool and dry)
Population: 16.5 million

URUGUAY
Capital: Montevideo
Area: 67,035 sq/miles
Climate: warm, temperate
Population: 3.5 million

Montevideo

Buenos Aires

Santiago

Argentina is the birthplace of the graceful dance, tango.

Fun Facts

Argentina's population is predominantly of European descent after a wave of European investment and immigration around 1870.

DID YOU KNOW?

When Paraguay and Bolivia fought a war in the 1930s, 36,000 Paraguayan soldiers lost their lives.

WESTERN EUROPE

Western Europe generally refers to the countries in the westermost half of Europe, although exact definitions vary.

It took eight years and more than 430 construction workers to build Tower Bridge, London.

London

Spain

Spain dominates most of the Iberian Peninsula in southwest Europe. The landscape is dominated by high plateaus with mountain ranges. The nation was a dominant force in Europe during the 16th and 17th centuries. Bull fighting remains a major attraction, despite increasing opposition to its cruelty.

FRANCE
Capital: Paris
Area: 210,669 sq/miles
Climate: cool winters and mild summers
Population: 64 million

Paris

The Eiffel Tower, Paris, is the tallest building in France and one of the world's most famous structures.

Lisbon

Madrid

Bullfighting is still passionately followed in Spain.

SPAIN
Capital: Madrid
Area: 192,874 sq/miles
Climate: temperate
Population: 41 million

The United Kingdom

The North Sea and the English Channel separate the United Kingdom from the rest of Europe. The countries of England, Scotland, Wales, and Northern Ireland make up the United Kingdom. England is the region's most populous area with 49 million inhabitants.

UNITED KINGDOM
Capital: London
Area: 93,278 sq/miles
Climate: temperate
Population: 61 million

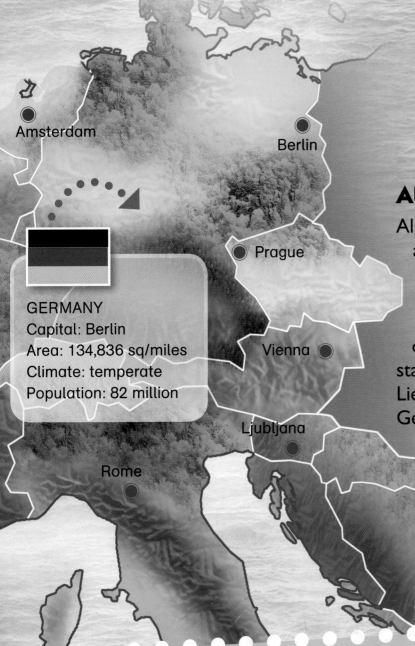

Amsterdam

Berlin

Prague

GERMANY
Capital: Berlin
Area: 134,836 sq/miles
Climate: temperate
Population: 82 million

Vienna

Ljubljana

Rome

Alpine countries

Alpine states refer to the countries associated with the Alps region. As defined by the Alpine Convention of 1991, the region of the Alps comprises of the territories of seven countries. These seven states of the Alps are Switzerland, Liechtenstein, Austria, Slovenia, Germany, France and Italy.

Fun Facts

Belgium is nicknamed 'the battlefield of Europe' and 'the cockpit of Europe' due to its strategic role in the World Wars.

DID YOU KNOW?

It is illegal to kill a bull in Portuguese bullfighting.

NORTHERN EUROPE

Northern Europe is a loose term that generally includes the Nordic countries of northernmost Europe, including: Sweden, Finland, Iceland, Denmark and Norway.

Norway

Norway is partitioned by mountains and has a fjord-rich shoreline that is over 13,050 miles (21,000 km) long. Its merchant and oil fleets are among the world's largest. This country of over 4.6 million boasts an extremely high literacy rate.

NORWAY
Capital: Oslo
Area: 118,704 sq/miles
Climate: temperate to cool
Population: 4.6 million

Finland

Finland, in northern Europe, has a mountainous landscape in the north and is low-lying in the center and the south. The population is mostly concentrated in the triangle formed by the cities of Tampere, Turku, and Helsinki. The country is home to over 180,000 lakes well complimented by rich coniferous forests.

Fun Facts

Denmark once controlled the whole of northern Europe and was a very important power. It is where the play *Hamlet* by William Shakespeare is set.

Sweden

Sweden is a highly successful and peaceful northern European country with high levels of literacy and employment. It is the third biggest country in the European Union by landmass, with about 85 percent of the people residing in urban areas. The landscape is mostly low and flat.

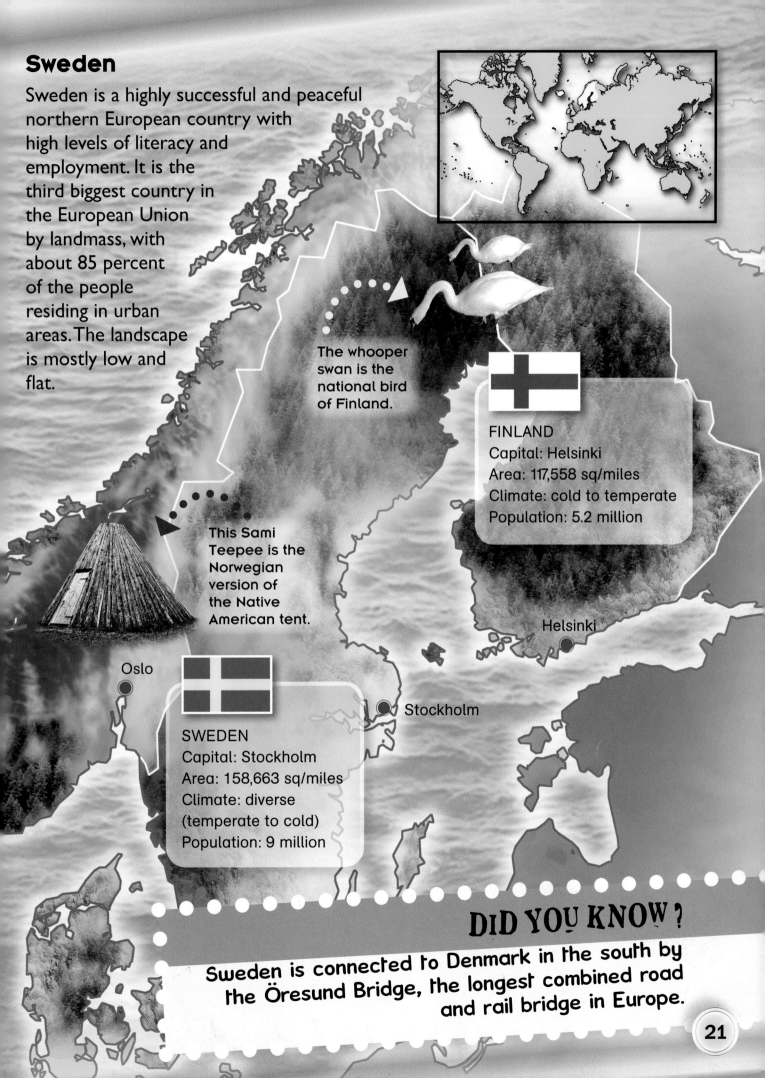

The whooper swan is the national bird of Finland.

This Sami Teepee is the Norwegian version of the Native American tent.

FINLAND
Capital: Helsinki
Area: 117,558 sq/miles
Climate: cold to temperate
Population: 5.2 million

Helsinki

Oslo

Stockholm

SWEDEN
Capital: Stockholm
Area: 158,663 sq/miles
Climate: diverse (temperate to cold)
Population: 9 million

DID YOU KNOW?

Sweden is connected to Denmark in the south by the Öresund Bridge, the longest combined road and rail bridge in Europe.

CENTRAL EUROPE

Central Europe is the region lying between the defined areas of Eastern and Western Europe. It includes the countries of Estonia, Latvia, Lithuania, Poland, Slovakia, Czech Republic and Hungary.

Czech Republic

The Czech Republic consists of the regions of Moravia and Bohemia. Moravia is mostly hills and lowlands and lies to the east; Bohemia is more of a plateau and is surrounded by mountains. The castles and palaces in the country are a wonderful attraction to tourists.

CZECH REPUBLIC
Capital: Prague
Area: 29,836 sq/miles
Climate: temperate
Population: 10.2 million

POLAND
Capital: Warsaw
Area: 117,552 sq/miles
Climate: temperate to cold
Population: 38.5 million

Prague

Warsaw

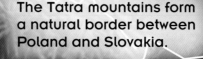

The Tatra mountains form a natural border between Poland and Slovakia.

Hungary

The Danube River flows north to south and cuts **landlocked** Hungary almost in half. The Hungarians migrated from Asia more than a thousand years ago. The culture is, thus, distinct from countries around it that are dominated by Germanic and Slavic peoples.

HUNGARY
Capital: Budapest
Area: 35,653 sq/miles
Climate: temperate
Population: 10 million

Budapest

Estonia

A republic in northeastern Europe on the Baltic Sea, Estonia is the smallest of the Baltic States. Curiously, it has the highest ratio of meteorite craters to land area in the world and it is also one of the most sparsely populated countries in Europe.

ESTONIA
Capital: Tallinn
Area: 16,684 sq/miles
Climate: moderate winters, temperate summers
Population: 1.3 million

Tallinn

Riga

Vilniusa

Riga in Latvia is well-known for its beautiful, distinctive architecture.

Fun Facts

The traditional houses in Slovakia, which are mostly wooden houses, are painted with designs based on traditional embroidery from the region.

Prague's astronomical clock is a popular tourist attraction.

DID YOU KNOW?

The white-tailed eagle is the national symbol of Poland.

SOUTHEASTERN EUROPE

The Balkan region in southeastern Europe takes its name from the Balkan Mountains, which run from Bulgaria into eastern Serbia.

Zagreb

Belgrade

CROATIA
Capital: Zagreb
Area: 21,782 sq/miles
Climate: **Mediterranean** and **continental**
Population: 4.5 million

Sarajevo

Greece

People have lived in Greece for more than 5,000 years. Its civilization started about 2,500 years ago. The country of Greece has many islands. Some of its earlier people wrote plays that are still performed today. Greece is also known for its sculptures.

Fun Facts

The ancient ritual of barefooted dancing on smoldering embers, emerged in several remote villages in the Strandzha Mountains, in Bulgaria.

Tirane

DID YOU KNOW?

Macedonia is the only part of the former Yugoslavia which won its independence without bloodshed. It was also the birthplace of Alexander the Great.

ROMANIA
Capital: Bucharest
Area: 88,935 sq/miles
Climate: temperate
Population: 22.2 million

The Bran castle is a national monument of Romania.

Bucharest

Sofia

BULGARIA
Capital: Sofia
Area: 42,684 sq/miles
Climate: temperate
Population: 7.2 million

GREECE
Capital: Athens
Area: 50,502 sq/miles
Climate: temperate
Population: 10.7 million

Athens

Romania

On the Black Sea coast of southeastern Europe lies the country of Romania. The country is divided into three major regions — Wallachia in the south, Moldavia in the northeast, and Transylvania at the center. Though the majority of the population is Romanian, there is a fair population of Hungarians too.

Slovenia

Slovenia is a state in central Europe and was once a part of Yugoslavia. Slovenia won its independence in June 1991, after a ten-day battle with the Yugoslav army. Of all the independent nations of the former Yugoslavia, Slovenia is the most prosperous, with the highest living standards.

The Parthenon in Athens, Greece.

25

NORTH AFRICA

Africa is the world's second-largest and second most-populated continent after Asia. North Africa is the northernmost region of the African continent, separated from the rest of Africa by the Sahara Desert.

Egypt

Egypt is one of the most populated countries in Africa and the Middle East. A great majority of the people live near the banks of the River Nile. Egypt is famous for its ancient civilization and some of the world's most famous monuments, including the pyramid of Giza and its Great Sphinx. The terrain is dominated by deserts. The east is home to mountainous deserts, and the west has a drier desert. The Sahara lies to the south.

Rabat

Tripoli

Dakar

Abuja

LIBYA
Capital: Tripoli
Area: 675,679 sq/miles
Climate: Mediterranean to dry
Population: 6.3 million

Camel trekking in North Africa.

Fun Facts

Although it is situated in North Africa, Morocco is the only African country that is presently not a member of the African Union.

EGYPT
Capital: Cairo
Area: 384,345 sq/miles
Climate: desert
Population: 83 million

The famous Sphinx and pyramids, Egypt.

○ Cairo

○ Khartoum

SUDAN
Capital: Khartoum
Area: 918,923 sq/miles
Climate: tropical to desert
Population: 41 million

○ Addis Ababa

ETHIOPIA
Capital: Addis Ababa
Area: 432,434 sq/miles
Climate: tropical monsoon
Population: 85 million

Sudan

Much of Sudan is a hot, dry place where nomads herd camels and sheep. Sudan's traditional dress, the jalabia, is a loose fitting robe well suited to desert conditions. It is usually worn with a large scarf and a thobe, which is a type of long shirt.

Libya

Libya is blessed with oil, but it lacks water. It is the country with the highest per capita income in the continent. The population is mainly concentrated in its two major cities, Tripoli and Banghazi. Libya's Great Man-Made River Project is the biggest of its kind in the world, helping the **coastal** cities get much-needed water.

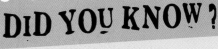

DID YOU KNOW?

Ethiopia is Africa's largest coffee producing country and the second largest producer of cut flowers in Africa.

CENTRAL AND SOUTHERN
AFRICA

Central Africa is the heart of the African continent. It includes Burundi, the Central African Republic, Chad, Republic of the Congo, and Rwanda. Southern Africa consists of the Republic of South Africa, Zimbabwe and Namibia.

Burundi

This small nation is located southeast of the equator. Though small in size, it has a dense population. Agriculture is the dominant occupation, with 90 percent of the population being farmers.

South Africa

The Republic of South Africa is a country located at the southern tip of the continent of Africa. South Africa is known for its great diversity in cultures, languages, religious beliefs and ethnic groups. For many years South Africa had a system of Apartheid, where racial groups were separated, but this was abolished in 1994, to great celebration worldwide.

REPUBLIC OF THE CONGO
Capital: Brazzaville
Area: 131,854 sq/miles
Climate: tropical
Population: 4 million

Fun Facts

The country of Rwanda has a hill-dominated landscape. Because of this, it is nicknamed the 'land of a thousand hills'.

DID YOU KNOW?

The presence of important minerals like cobalt, copper, diamonds, gold, silver, tin and coltan makes the Congo one of Africa's most mineral-rich countries.

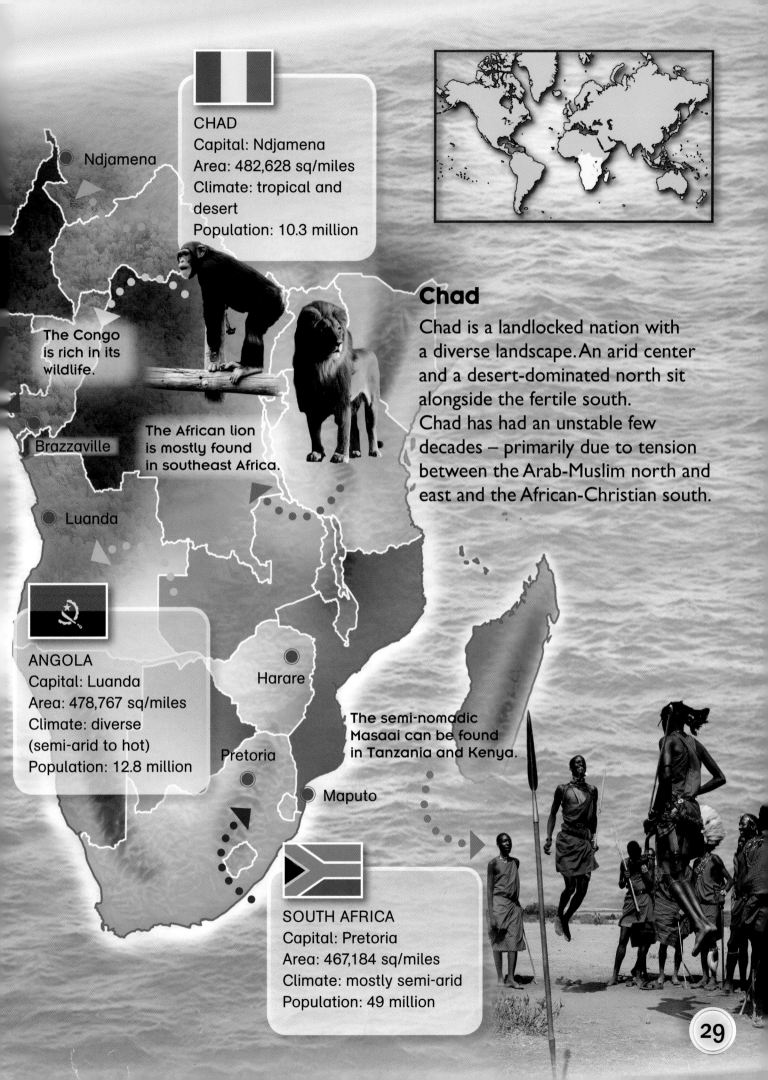

CHAD
Capital: Ndjamena
Area: 482,628 sq/miles
Climate: tropical and desert
Population: 10.3 million

Ndjamena

The Congo is rich in its wildlife.

Brazzaville

The African lion is mostly found in southeast Africa.

Luanda

Chad

Chad is a landlocked nation with a diverse landscape. An arid center and a desert-dominated north sit alongside the fertile south.
Chad has had an unstable few decades – primarily due to tension between the Arab-Muslim north and east and the African-Christian south.

ANGOLA
Capital: Luanda
Area: 478,767 sq/miles
Climate: diverse (semi-arid to hot)
Population: 12.8 million

Harare

The semi-nomadic Masaai can be found in Tanzania and Kenya.

Pretoria

Maputo

SOUTH AFRICA
Capital: Pretoria
Area: 467,184 sq/miles
Climate: mostly semi-arid
Population: 49 million

MIDDLE EAST

The Middle East spans the whole of southwestern Asia and northeastern Africa. It has a dry and hot climate. Countries in the Middle East include Iraq, Iran, Israel, UAE, Kuwait and Jordan.

The Western, or Wailing Wall is one of the most sacred places for people of Jewish faith.

Jerusalem   Amman

ISRAEL
Capital: Jerusalem
Area: 7,849 sq/miles
Climate: temperate
Population: 7.2 million

JORDAN
Capital: Amman
Area: 35,510 sq/miles
Climate: mostly arid
Population: 6.3 million

Iran

Iran is a country full of mountains and deserts. Desert areas dominate the east of the country. Farming is primarily concentrated in the narrow plains or valleys in the north and west – places more likely to get rainfall. The oil reserves lie in the southwest.

Mecca is considered the center of the Islamic faith.

Israel

The eastern interior of Israel is dry and includes the lowest point on the Earth's surface – the Dead Sea. The majority of the population is Jewish, with a minority Arab population.

Fun Facts

Iran is one of the world's oldest continuous major civilizations, with historical and urban settlements dating back to 4,000 BC.

Tehran

IRAN
Capital: Tehran
Area: 629,347 sq/miles
Climate: mostly arid and semi-arid
Population: 66 million

Kuwait City

Riyadh

KUWAIT
Capital: Kuwait City
Area: 6,880 sq/miles
Climate: dry and hot
Population: 2.6 million

Jordan

The country of Jordan is dominated by desert plateaus and is largely landlocked but for a short coast. Jordan lacks in natural resources – surprisingly, it does not have its own oil. Jordan has seen an influx of Palestinian refugees as a result of the Israeli-Palestinian conflict.

Abu Dhabi

The rock-cut architecture of the Petra in Jordan is known as one of the new wonders of the world.

DID YOU KNOW ?

Kuwait was the first Arab country in the Gulf to have an elected parliament.

31

RUSSIA AND NEIGHBORING COUNTRIES

Russia is the largest country in the world in terms of area. Its neighbors include Kazakhstan, Turkmenistan, Ukraine, Moldova, and Uzbekistan, among others.

The majestic but endangered Siberian tiger.

RUSSIA
Capital: Moscow
Area: 6.56 million sq/miles
Climate: Diverse (warm to extremely cold)
Population: 140 million

Moscow

The St. Basil's Cathedral is about 450 years old.

Russia

Founded in the 12ᵗʰ century, Russia established worldwide power and influence to become the largest socialist state and a recognized superpower. Russia has many attractions, from freshwater lakes, soaring mountains, rivers and forests to beautiful and rich wildlife.

KAZAKHSTAN
Capital: Astana
Area: 1.03 million sq/miles
Climate: continental
Population: 15.3 million

Kazakh people can be found in China and Mongolia as well.

Astana

UZBEKISTAN
Capital: Tashkent
Area: 164,248 sq/miles
Climate: hot summers, mild winters
Population: 27.5 million

Bishkek

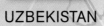
Tashkent

Kazakhstan

Kazakhstan is a country in central Asia and Eastern Europe. It is ranked as the ninth largest country in the world as well as the world's largest landlocked country. Kazakhstan is famous for the Baykonur Cosmodrome or space station.

Uzbekistan

Uzbekistan is central Asia's most populated nation. About 80 percent of the country is dominated by the Qizilqum desert, with mountain ranges present in the southeast and the northeast of the country. The Fergana Valley lies to the country's northeast and is its most developed and fertile region, containing many industries.

The brown bear is one of the top predators in the jungles of Russia.

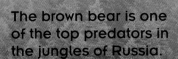
Russia is famous for its ballet.

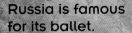

Fun Facts

The Voronya Cave, situated in Georgia, is the deepest known cave in the world.

DID YOU KNOW?

Armenia is home to a leading center of metallurgy, the scientific study of metal and its properties.

CHINA AND NEIGHBORING COUNTRIES

China is the most populous country in the world and one of the biggest. Its neighbors include Japan, Singapore, Mongolia and Cambodia, among others.

Ulan Bator ●

The home to the nomadic Mongol.

CHINA
Capital: Beijing
Area: 3.6 million sq/miles
Climate: diverse (tropical to very cold)
Population: 1.3 billion

China

China is the third largest country in the world. It is also one of the world's oldest civilizations with a history of more than 7,000 years. The landscape is diverse, with hills, plains, mountains, and deltas. The climate ranges from hot tropical in the south to subarctic in the northeast.

Paddy fields — a feature of rice-growing China.

Fun Facts

Mongolia is the seventh largest country in Asia in terms of area. The country is totally landlocked, with China on one side and Russia on the other.

South Korea

South Korea comprises the southern half of the Korean peninsula, and numerous islands off the southern and western coasts. The landscape is full of mountains, though less in number than in North Korea.

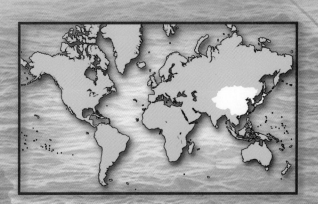

China's great wall can be seen from the moon.

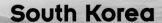

Beijing

P'yongyang

Seoul

JAPAN
Capital: Tokyo
Area: 144,689 sq/miles
Climate: tropical to cool
Population: 127 million

Tokyo

SOUTH KOREA
Capital: Seoul
Area: 37,911 sq/miles
Climate: temperate
Population: 48 million

Shanghai

Japan

Japan is an island country in East Asia. The ancient Japanese people believed theirs was the first land awakened by the rising sun. The Japanese call their land Nippon, meaning 'land of the rising sun'. It is believed that only 18 percent of Japan's land is suitable for **settlement**, which explains the over-populated cites!

Taipei

DID YOU KNOW?

In the Gobi Desert of Mongolia fossilized dinosaur remains were found in 1920s, as well as the first dinosaur egg.

THE INDIAN SUBCONTINENT

The subcontinent comprises India, Pakistan, Nepal, Bhutan, Bangladesh and Sri Lanka.

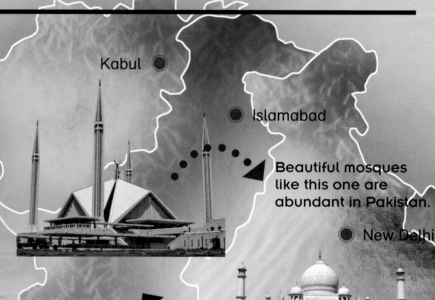

Kabul

Islamabad

Beautiful mosques like this one are abundant in Pakistan.

New Delhi

PAKISTAN
Capital: Islamabad
Area: 300,665 sq/miles
Climate: mostly hot
Population: 176 million

The Taj Mahal is one of India's most beautiful monuments.

Mumbai

India

India is the biggest country in the subcontinent and has the second largest population in the world. India's physical, religious and racial variety is reflected in its culture. This vast cultural diversity is reflected in its religious **monuments** – temple, mosques, churches, monasteries, gurudwaras etc.

INDIA
Capital: New Delhi
Area: 1.15 million sq/miles
Climate: tropical monsoon to temperate
Population: 1.1 billion

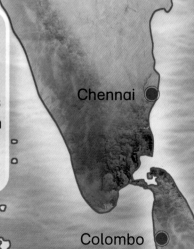

Chennai

Colombo

Pakistan

The eastern and southern parts of the country have the Indus River and its tributaries; most of the population is concentrated along these areas. West of the river, the land is dry and mountainous. To the north lies K2, the tallest mountain in the world after Everest.

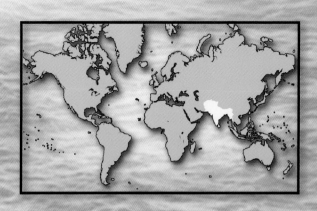

Fun Facts

Many of the houses in Bangladesh are often raised on stilts or embankments to help protect them from flooding.

Sri Lanka

Sri Lanka is a tropical island nation that lies at the southernmost tip of India. Most of the well-renowned tea plantations are found at the center of the country. The Sinhalese community constitutes the majority of the population, while the Tamils dominate the minority. The southwest is the most densely populated, and it is here that you can find Colombo, the country's capital.

Dhaka

Kolkata

BANGLADESH
Capital: Dhaka
Area: 43,981 sq/miles
Climate: tropical
Population: 156 million

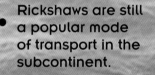

Rickshaws are still a popular mode of transport in the subcontinent.

DID YOU KNOW?

Eight of the highest peaks of the world, including Mount Everest, are situated in Nepal.

SOUTHEAST ASIA

Southeast Asia lies south of China, east of India and north of Australia. The region is known for earthquakes and tremors (seismic activity) because several geological plates meet here.

Hanoi

THAILAND
Capital: Bangkok
Area: 197,596 sq/miles
Climate: tropical
Population: 66 million

VIETNAM
Capital: Hanoi
Area: 125,622 sq/miles
Climate: diverse (tropical to dry)
Population: 87 million

Thailand

The Chao Phraya River basin dominates the country of Thailand. Bangkok, the country's capital, lies in this basin. East Thailand is mainly woodlands and grasses. The southern region is full of hills and is well forested. Northern Thailand has the highest mountains.

Bangkok

Phnom Penh

The Petronas Towers are two of the tallest buildings in the world.

MALAYSIA
Capital: Kuala Lumpur
Area: 126,854 sq/miles
Climate: tropical
Population: 26 million

Kuala Lumpur

Vietnam

Vietnam is 1,000 miles (1,600 km) long from north to south and is extremely narrow – just 25 miles (40 km) wide at its narrowest. The Red River and the Mekong River dominate the landscape. Hanoi is the main city of the Red River, and Ho Chi Minh is the main city of the Mekong River.

Cambodia

Cambodia is mostly covered with forests. Once a war zone in the latter half of the 20th century, the country enjoys greater stability these days. **Subsistence farming** is still the predominant means of earning.

Manila

Fun Facts

The Petronas Towers in Malaysia are the world's tallest twin buildings and were the tallest buildings in the world until Taipei 101 was built.

An exotic Bali dancer.

DID YOU KNOW?

Indonesia is a transcontinental country spanning Southeast Asia and Oceania, comprised of more than 17,000 islands!

AUSTRALIA AND NEIGHBORING COUNTRIES

Australia is a country in the southern hemisphere. Australasian countries include New Zealand, East Timor, Solomon Islands and Papua New Guinea.

Settlement in Australia

Aboriginal settlers arrived on the continent from Southeast Asia about 40,000 years before the first Europeans began exploration in the 17th century. Six colonies were created in the late 18th and 19th centuries. Today, Australia is one of the most popular destinations for tourists.

Papua New Guinea

Papua New Guinea, in the Southwest Pacific, is one of the most diverse countries in the world. This largely unexplored nation has over 850 indigenous languages.

AUSTRALIA
Capital: Canberra
Area: 2.9 million sq/miles
Climate: arid to semi-arid
Population: 21 million

The red kangaroo is the national animal of Australia.

● Perth

DID YOU KNOW?

The world's largest saltwater lagoon, Marovo Lagoon, is situated in New Georgia, Solomon Islands.

PAPUA NEW GUINEA
Capital: Port Morseby
Area: 174,850 sq/miles
Climate: tropical
Population: 6 million

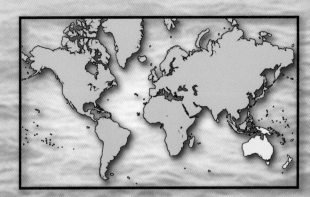

SOLOMON ISLANDS
Capital: Honiara
Area: 10,663 sq/miles
Climate: tropical
monsoon
Population: 600,000

Rugby, the country's national game, is followed passionately in New Zealand.

The Sydney Opera House stages up to 2,500 art performances and events each year.

Sydney

Canberra

New Zealand

New Zealand is an island country in the south-western Pacific Ocean. It has two main landmasses, the North Island and the South Island, and numerous smaller islands. The original Maori inhabitants named New Zealand Aotearoa, meaning 'the land of the long white cloud'. The indigenous, flightless kiwi is the country's national bird.

Melbourne

Hobart

NEW ZEALAND
Capital: Wellington
Area: 103,483 sq/miles
Climate: temperate
Population: 4.2 million

Wellington

THE POLES AND GREENLAND

The Earth, like a magnet, has two poles – the North Pole and the South Pole. These regions are dominated by the polar ice-caps, resting on the Arctic Ocean and the continent of Antarctica.

North Pole

The Earth's North Pole is covered by a floating pack of ice over the Arctic Ocean. The land from the North Pole down to the northern forests is known as the Tundra. Despite the extreme climate, animals that survive and make the Tundra their home include polar bears, Arctic hares and Arctic foxes.

The fur of the Arctic fox turns grey-brown during summer.

The polar bear is an accomplished swimmer and is often found at sea.

GREENLAND
Capital: Nuuk
Area: 833,980 sq/miles
Climate: extreme cold
Population: 57,600

South Pole

The landmass of the Earth's South Pole (or Antarctica) is covered by the Antarctic ice sheet. Seventy percent of the fresh water on Earth can be found in this ice sheet. The South Pole is much colder than the North Pole as it receives less solar radiation.

Greenland

Greenland is one of the world's largest islands, but it is not classified as a continent. Geographically a part of North America, its history is dominated by Denmark, Norway and Iceland.

The penguin is one of the few living creatures thriving in the Antarctic.

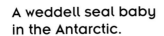

A weddell seal baby in the Antarctic.

Fun Facts

There are no permanent human residents in Antarctica because of the freezing cold.

DID YOU KNOW?

Less rain falls annually in Antarctica than in the Sahara Desert!

GLOSSARY

Biodiversity: range of plants and animals living in a specific area

Coastal: relating to or of a coast

Continental: something typical of mainland Europe

Diverse: different and many

Earth: planet where we live

Himalayas: a 1,500 mile (2,400 km) mountain range in India and Tibet

Indigenous: originating where it was found

Landlocked: surrounded by land

Landscape: all the visible features of an area

Mediterranean: related to or near the Mediterranean Sea

Monuments: historical structures

Natural Resource: resources found in nature

Rockies: mountain range of western North America

Settlement: area where a group of people live together

Subsistence farming: farming that produces food enough for a farmer's family

INDEX